MY CARAVAN

How lucky the gipsies are.
With holidays all in a row,
And never a guide but a star,
And ever a road to go!
—*Katharine Lee Bates*

MY CARAVAN

A Book of Poems for Boys and Girls

in Search of Adventure

Edited by

EULALIE OSGOOD GROVER

Author of "The Sunbonnet Baby"

and "The Overall Boy"

Books

Illustrated with

Cut-paper Silhouettes by

FLORENCE SAMPSON

GRANGER BOOKS
MIAMI, FLORIDA

FIRST PUBLISHED 1931
REPRINTED 1976

PRINTED IN THE UNITED STATES OF AMERICA

THE CARAVAN'S TRAIL

Here is a book of real adventure for girls and boys—adventure found only on the Magic Trail of Poetry.

The Trail leads wherever the fancy may go—down the long road with the wandering Caravan, *with a horse to drive, like a peddler-man,* or *up the airy mountain and down the rushy glen,* or it may even lead to the *shining hillsides of the moon,* where wonderful dreams—*pleasant and dreadful and gay and queer are piled in a silver heap.*

This world of our fancy is strange and adventurous, and only the roving poet knows how to guide us happily through it, for *after all, and after all, great adventures may befall, like to those that happened once, long and long ago.*

From cover design to the last end-paper, the pictures in this book have been cut with Magic Scissors from bits of black or sometimes white paper. With the help of these Scissors, the whimsy artist has created gipsies and fairies and happy children to be your companions along the Magic Trail.

The gate to this Trail is wide open. The Caravan is waiting. Are you ready for the adventure?

—*E. O. G.*

THE CONTENTS

I GO ADVENTURING

OUT-OF-DOORS

THE FAIRY FOLK

8

JUST FOR FUN

SHADOW TIME

I GO ADVENTURING

If I could be a gipsy-boy
And have a caravan,
I'd travel all the world, I would,
Before I was a man.

—*Madeleine Nightingale*

THE PEDDLER'S CARAVAN

I wish I lived in a caravan,
With a horse to drive, like a peddler-man!
Where he comes from nobody knows,
Or where he goes to, but on he goes!

His caravan has windows two,
And a chimney of tin, that the smoke comes through;
He has a wife, with a baby brown,
And they go riding from town to town.

Chairs to mend, and delf to sell!
He clashes the basins like a bell;
Tea-trays, baskets ranged in order,
Plates with the alphabet round the border!

The roads are brown, and the sea is green,
But his house is just like a bathing-machine;
The world is round, and he can ride,
Rumble and splash, to the other side!

With the peddler-man I should like to roam,
And write a book when I come home;
All the people would read my book,
Just like the Travels of Captain Cook!

—*William Brighty Rands*

15

THE EDGE OF THE WORLD

From the top of the bluff, where the wind blows free,
Clear out to the edge of the world I see,
And I look and look, till my eyes grow dim,
But I can't see what lies over the rim!

I see the steamers go in towards town;
I watch the schooners sail slowly down—
Down out of sight, and far away—
Oh! I shall sail over the rim, some day.

Over the rim and far beyond,
To Hong-Kong and Bagdad and Trebizond,
And Ceylon's Isle, where the breezes blow,
And the Happy Harbor, where good ships go.

And it may be bad, or it may be fair,
And I may come back, or I may stay there,
But one thing is sure—be it gay or grim,
Some day—some day—I must cross that rim!

—*Mary Fanny Youngs*

16

MY SHIP AND I

Oh, it's I that am the captain of a tidy little ship,
Of a ship that goes a-sailing on the pond;
And my ship it keeps a-turning all around and all
　　about;
But when I'm a little older, I shall find the secret out—
How to send my vessel sailing on beyond.

For I mean to grow as little as the dolly at the helm,
And the dolly I intend to come alive;
And with him beside to help me, it's a-sailing I
　　shall go,
It's a-sailing on the water, when the jolly breezes blow,
And the vessel goes a divie-divie-dive.

Oh, it's then you'll see me sailing through the rushes
　　and the reeds,
And you'll hear the water singing at the prow;
For beside the dolly sailor, I'm to voyage and explore,
To land upon the island where no dolly was before,
And to fire the penny cannon in the bow.
　　　　　　　　　　　　—*Robert Louis Stevenson*

Adventuring Bees

A BEE SETS SAIL

The wind blows east, the wind blows storm,
And yet this very hour
I saw a bumblebee embark
In frigate of a flower;

An admiral in epaulets,
He strode the scented deck,
And in the teeth of tossing gales
He rode without a wreck.

More valorous adventurer
I never hope to see—
Though mariners be gallant men—
Than that same bumblebee.

—*Katharine Morse*

18

PAPER BOATS

Day by day I float my paper boats one by one down the running stream.

In big black letters I write my name on them and the name of the village where I live.

I hope that some one in some strange land will find them and know who I am.

I load my little boats with *shiuli* flowers from our garden, and hope that these blooms of dawn will be carried safely to land in the night.

I launch my paper boats and look up into the sky and see the little clouds setting their white bulging sails.

I know not what playmate of mine in the sky sends them down the air to race with my boats.

When night comes I bury my face in my arms and dream that my paper boats float on and on under the midnight stars.

The fairies of sleep are sailing in them, and the lading is their baskets full of dreams.

—*Rabindranath Tagore*

Up About the Polar Sea

AROUND THE WORLD

'Most every evening after tea,
I travel far as far can be;
I grasp the wheel with both my hands,
And soon I'm off for foreign lands.

I see all countries that I can:
Alaska, China, and Japan,
Then round by Italy and Spain,
And very soon I'm home again.

Then up about the Polar Sea,
Where bears and walrus stare at me.

20

At other times I take my way
To distant Burma and Malay.

In every land, down to the sea,
The people rush to look at me.
"Good luck to you," I hear them say;
I wave my hand and speed away.

Our dining-room is everywhere;
My ship is just a rocking-chair;
I cruise about the world, at sea,
'Most every evening after tea.

—*Thomas Tapper*

BOATS SAIL ON THE RIVERS

Boats sail on the rivers,
And ships sail on the seas;
But clouds that sail across the sky
Are prettier far than these.

There are bridges on the rivers,
As pretty as you please;
But the bow that bridges heaven,
And overtops the trees,
And builds a road from earth to sky,
Is prettier far than these.

—*Christina Rossetti*

21

THE CARAVAN

If I could be a gipsy-boy and have a caravan,
I'd travel all the world, I would, before I was a man;
We'd drive beyond the far blue hills—us two, my
    horse and me—
And on and on and on and on, until we reached the sea.

And there I'd wash his legs quite clean and bid him
    come inside,
While I would stand upon the roof and scan the flow-
    ing tide,
And he and I would sail away and scour the Spanish
    main,
And when we'd swept the Spaniards out, we'd p'r'aps
    sail home again.

Or if my horse was very tired of ships and being good,
And wanted most to stretch his legs (as many horses
    would),
We'd call a whale to tow us to a desert island beach,
And there we'd search for cocoanuts and have a whole
    one each.

If I could be a gipsy-boy, I wouldn't bring a load
Of pots and pans and chairs and things to sell them
    in the road.

Oh, if I were a gipsy-boy and had a caravan,
I'd see the whole wide world, I would, before I was a
    man.

—*Madeleine Nightingale*

OFF TO THE COUNTRY

We're off to the country,—one, two, three,
Solly and Molly Levitsky and me.
They've washed our faces and combed our hair;
We've on our cleanest and best to wear;
We're going to be as good as we can,
And live for a week with a farmer man.

We're hoping to see a real live cow,
A sheep and some chickens, and maybe learn how
To work in the fields and rake the hay
Out in the sunshine all the day.
We've heard there's plenty of room out there,
And bees and butterflies in the air.
I've seen a butterfly in a book—
The "library teacher" told where to look.

We're off to the country,—one, two, three,
Solly and Molly Levitsky and me.

—*Mary Elizabeth Rodhouse*

AT THE SEASIDE

When I was down beside the sea
A wooden spade they gave to me
To dig the sandy shore.
My holes were empty like a cup,
In every hole the sea came up,
Till it could come no more.

—*Robert Louis Stevenson*

ADVENTURE

I went slowly through the wood of shadows,
Thinking always I should meet some one:
There was no one.

I found a hollow
Sweet to rest in all night long:
I did not stay.

I came out beyond the trees
To the moaning sea.
Over the sea swam a cloud the outline of a ship:
What if that ship held my adventure
Under its sails?

24

My Ship of Adventure

Come quickly to me, come quickly,
I am waiting;
I am here on the sand.
Sail close!
I want to go over the waves . . .
The sand holds me back.
Oh adventure, if you belong to me,
Don't blow away down the sky!

—*Hilda Conkling*
(Written at nine years of age)

25

MOCKERY

Happened that the moon was up before I went to bed,
Poking through the bramble-trees her round, gold
    head.
I didn't stop for stocking,
I didn't stop for shoe,
But went running out to meet her—oh, the night was
    blue!

Barefoot down the hill road, dust beneath my toes;
Barefoot in the pasture smelling sweet of fern and rose!
Oh, night was running with me,
Tame folk were all in bed—
And the moon was just showing her wild, gold head!

But before I reached the hilltop, where the bramble-
    trees are tall,
I looked to see my lady moon—she wasn't there at
    all!—
Not sitting on the hilltop,
Nor slipping through the air,
Nor hanging in the brambles by her bright, gold hair!

I walked slowly down the pasture and slowly up the
    hill,
Wondering and wondering, and very, very, still.

I wouldn't look behind me,
I went at once to bed—
And poking through the window was her bold, gold
     head!

—*Katherine Dixon Riggs*

PIRATE STORY

Three of us afloat in the meadow by the swing.
Three of us aboard in the basket on the lea.
Winds are in the air, they are blowing in the spring,
And waves are on the meadow like the waves there
     are at sea.

Where shall we adventure, to-day that we're afloat,
Wary of the weather and steering by a star?
Shall it be to Africa, a-steering of the boat,
To Providence, or Babylon, or off to Malabar?

Hi! but here's a squadron a-rowing on the sea—
Cattle on the meadow a-charging with a roar!
Quick, and we'll escape them; they're as mad as they
     can be,
The wicket is the harbor and the garden is the shore.

—*Robert Louis Stevenson*

OVER THE HILL

"Traveler, what lies over the hill?
Traveler, tell me.
I am only a child—from the window-sill
Over I cannot see."

"Child, there's a valley over there,
Pretty and wooded and shy;
And a little brook that says, 'Take care,
Or you'll fall in by-and-by!' "

"And what comes next?" "A little town,
And a towering hill again;
More hills and valleys up and down,
And a river now and then."

"And what comes next?" "A lonely moor
Without a beaten way;
And gray clouds sailing slow before
A wind that will not stay."

"And then?" "Oh, dark rocks and yellow sand,
And a moaning sea beside."
"And then?" "More sea, more sea, more land,
And rivers deep and wide."

"And then?" "Oh, rock and mountain and vale,
Rivers and fields and men,
Over and over—a weary tale—
And round to your home again."

—George Macdonald

ON THE BRIDGE

If I could see a little fish—
That is what I just now wish!
I want to see his great round eyes
Always open in surprise.

I wish a water-rat would glide
Slowly to the other side;
Or a dancing spider sit
On the yellow flags a bit.

I think I'll get some stones to throw,
And watch the pretty circles show.
Or shall we sail a flower-boat,
And watch it slowly—slowly float?

That's nice—because you never know
How far away it means to go;
And when to-morrow comes, you see,
It may be in the great wide sea.

—Kate Greenaway

WHERE GO THE BOATS

Dark brown is the river,
Golden is the sand.
It flows along forever,
With trees on either hand.

Green leaves a-floating,
Castles of the foam,
Boats of mine a-boating—
Where will all come home?

On goes the river
And out past the mill,
Away down the valley,
Away down the hill.

Away down the river,
A hundred miles or more,
Other little children
Shall bring my boats ashore.

—Robert Louis Stevenson

OUT-OF-DOORS

I shall climb a green hill,
With summer winds above it;
And shall loose my chestnut hair;
And I shall love it!

—Winifred Gray Stewart

SUMMER RAPTURE

I shall climb a green hill,
With summer winds above it;
And shall loose my chestnut hair;
And I shall love it!

Oh, I shall climb a green hill,
With clover blossoms scented;
And weave a garland frail and fair;
And be contented!

Oh, I shall climb a green hill,
And when I reach the summit,
I'll find a little song there;
And I shall hum it!

—*Winifred Gray Stewart*

HAPPY THOUGHT

The world is so full of a number of things,
I'm sure we should all be as happy as kings.

—*Robert Louis Stevenson*

A RUNE OF RICHES

I have a golden ball,
A big, bright, shining one,
Pure gold; and it is all
Mine.—It is the sun.

I have a silver ball,
A white and glittering stone
That other people call
The moon;—my very own!

The jewel things that prick
My cushion's soft blue cover
Are mine,—my stars, thick, thick,
Scattered the sky all over.

And everything that's mine
Is yours, and yours, and yours,—
The shimmer and the shine!—
Let's lock our wealth out-doors!

—*Florence Converse*

34

SUNSET AND SUNRISE

I'll tell you how the sun rose,—
A ribbon at a time.
The steeples swam in amethyst,
The news like squirrels ran.

The hills untied their bonnets,
The bobolinks begun.
Then I said softly to myself,
"That must have been the sun!"

. . . . . .

But how it set, I know not.
There seemed a purple stile
Which little yellow boys and girls
Were climbing all the while.

Till when they reached the other side,
A dominie in gray
Put gently up the evening bars,
And led the flock away.

—*Emily Dickinson*

35

SONG FROM "APRIL"

I know
Where the wind flowers blow!
I know,
I have been
Where the wild honey bees
Gather honey for their queen!

I would be
A wild flower,
Blue sky over me
For an hour . . . an hour!
So the wild bees
Should seek and discover me,
And kiss me . . . kiss me . . kiss me!
Not one of the dusky dears should miss me!

I know
Where the wind flowers blow!
I know,
I have been
Where the little rabbits run
In the warm, yellow sun!

Where the Little Rabbits Run

Oh, to be a wild flower
For an hour . . . an hour . . .
In the heather!
A bright flower, a wild flower,
Blown by the weather!

I know,
I have been
Where the wild honey bees
Gather honey for their queen!

—*Irene Rutherford McLeod*

WHO CALLS?

"Listen, children, listen, won't you come into the
    night?
The stars have set their candle gleam, the moon her
    lanthorn light.
I'm piping little tunes for you to catch your dancing
    feet.
There's glory in the heavens, but there's magic in the
    street.
There's jesting here and carnival: the cost of a balloon
Is an ancient rhyme said backwards, and a wish upon
    the moon.
The city walls and city streets!—you shall make of
    these
As fair a thing as country roads and blossomy apple
    trees."

"What watchman calls us in the night, and plays a
    little tune
That turns our tongues to talking now of April, May
    and June?
Who bids us come with nimble feet and snapping
    finger tips?"

"I am Spring, the Spring, the Spring with laughter on
    my lips."

—*Frances Clarke*

38

MARCH

I wonder what spendthrift chose to spill
Such bright gold under my window-sill!
Is it fairy gold? Does it glitter still?
Bless me! It is but a daffodil!

And look at the crocuses keeping tryst
With the daffodil by the sunshine kissed!
Like beautiful bubbles of amethyst,
They seem, blown out of the earth's snow-mist.

O March that blusters, and March that blows,
What color under your footstep glows!
Beauty you summon from winter snows,
And you are the pathway that leads to the rose.

—*Celia Thaxter*

A SPRING MESSAGE

I heard the rain fall in the night;
Softly it fell,
Slowly, carelessly,
And I knew
That everywhere little brown doors were opening,
That everywhere little green things were stepping
Shyly, daintily,
Over the threshold of Spring.

—*Joan Alpermann*

APRIL RAIN

It is not raining rain to me,
It's raining daffodils;
In every dimpled drop I see
Wild flowers on the hills.

The clouds of gray engulf the day
And overwhelm the town;
It is not raining rain to me,
It's raining roses down.

It is not raining rain to me,
But fields of clover bloom,
Where any buccaneering bee
Can find a bed and room.

A health unto the happy,
A fig for him who frets!
It is not raining rain to me,
It's raining violets.

—Robert Loveman

SOME ONE

Some one came knocking
  At my wee, small door;
Some one came knocking,
  I'm sure—sure—sure;
I listened, I opened,
  I looked to left and right,
But nought there was a-stirring
  In the still, dark night;
Only the busy beetle
  Tap-tapping in the wall,
Only from the forest
  The screech-owl's call,
Only the cricket whistling
  While the dewdrops fall.
So I know not who came knocking,
  At all, at all, at all.

—*Walter de la Mare*

41

Spring

FOUR DUCKS ON A POND

Four ducks on a pond,
A grass-bank beyond,
A blue sky of spring,
White clouds on the wing—
What a little thing
To remember for years!
To remember with tears!

—*William Allingham*

THE THROSTLE

"Summer is coming, summer is coming,
  I know it, I know it, I know it.
Light again, leaf again, life again, love again,"
  Yes, my wild little Poet.

Sing the new year in under the blue.
  Last year you sang it as gladly.
"New, new, new, new!" Is it then so new
  That you should carol so madly?

"Love again, song again, nest again, young again,"
  Never a prophet so crazy!
And hardly a daisy as yet, little friend,
  See, there is hardly a daisy.

"Here again, here, here, here, happy year!"
  Oh, warble unchidden, unbidden!
Summer is coming, is coming, my dear,
  And all the winters are hidden.

—*Alfred Tennyson*

43

FOUR AND EIGHT

The Foxglove by the cottage door
Looks down on Joe, and Joe is Four.

The Foxglove by the garden gate
Looks down on Joan, and Joan is Eight.

"I'm glad we're small," said Joan, "I love
To see inside the fox's glove,
Where taller people cannot see,
And all is ready for the bee;
The door is wide, the feast is spread,
The walls are dotted rosy red;"
"And only little people know
How nice it looks in there," said Joe.
Said Joan, "The upper rooms are locked;
A bee went buzzing up—he knocked,
But no one let him in, so then
He bumbled gaily down again."
"Oh, dear!" sighed Joe, "if only we
Could grow as little as that bee,
We, too, might room by room explore
The Foxglove by the cottage door."

The Foxglove by the garden gate
Looked down and smiled on Four and Eight.

—*Ffrida Wolfe*

PLAYGROUNDS

In summer I am very glad
We children are so small,
For we can see a thousand things
That men can't see at all.

They don't know much about the moss
And all the stones they pass;
They never lie and play among
The forests in the grass;

They walk about a long way off;
And when we're at the sea,
Let father stoop as best he can
He can't find things like me.

. . . . . .

—*Laurence Alma-Tadema*

SONG

The year's at the spring,
And day's at the morn;
Morning's at seven;
The hill-side's dew-pearled;
The lark's on the wing;
The snail's on the thorn;
God's in His Heaven—
All's right with the world!

—*Robert Browning*

I Am the Dancer of the Wood

THE SPIRIT OF THE BIRCH

I am the dancer of the wood—
I shimmer in the solitude;
Men call me Birch Tree, yet I know
In other days it was not so.
I am a Dryad slim and white
Who danced too long one summer night,
And the Dawn found and prisoned me!
Captive I moaned my liberty.
But let the wood wind flutes begin
Their elfin music, faint and thin,
I sway, I bend, retreat, advance,
And evermore—I dance! I dance!

—*Arthur Ketchum*

46

THE ALL ALONE TREE

There's a tree that is growing alone on the hill,
By the path that winds up at the back of the mill,
And we're awfully fond of it, Maudie and me,
And we call it the All Alone, All Alone Tree.

It is old, and it's wrinkled and twisted and dry,
And it grows by itself with no other tree nigh,
And we always sit under it, Maudie and me,
Because it's the All Alone, All Alone Tree.

In the bright summer-time when they're cutting the
    hay,
Then the birds come and sing in its branches all day,
And we're awfully glad of this, Maudie and me,
Because it's the All Alone, All Alone Tree.

But in the dark winter the birds have all flown,
And we know that it's standing there, quite, **quite**
    alone,
So we creep out and kiss it then, Maudie and me,
Because it's the All Alone, All Alone Tree.

—F. O'Neill Galligher

THE RIVULET

Run, little rivulet, run!
Summer is fairly begun.
Bear to the meadow the hymn of the pines,
And the echo that rings where the waterfall shines;
Run, little rivulet, run!

Run, little rivulet, run!
Sing to the fields of the sun
That wavers in emerald, shimmers in gold,
Where you glide from your rocky ravine, crystal-cold;
Run, little rivulet, run!

Run, little rivulet, run!
Sing of the flowers, every one, —
Of the delicate harebell and violet blue;
Of the red mountain rose-bud, all dripping with dew;
Run, little rivulet, run!

. . . . . .

Run, little rivulet, run!
Stay not till summer is done!
Carry the city the mountain-birds' glee;
Carry the joy of the hills to the sea;
Run, little rivulet, run!

—*Lucy Larcom*

MY GARDEN

When I've hoed and dug my garden
All the day,
When I've put my spade and barrow
Safe away,
When I've said good-night to my garden,
When all my prayers are said,
I know that God will watch my garden,
When I am safe in bed.

When I wake and find my happy garden
Fresh and sweet,
When the diamond dew is shining
Round my feet,
When all the buds of yesterday
Are blossoms blooming bright,
I know that God has watched my garden
And blessed it all the night.

—*Fred E. Weatherly*

SUMMER DAYS

Winter is cold-hearted;
Spring is yea and nay;
Autumn is a weathercock,
Blown every way;
Summer days for me,
When every leaf is on its tree,

When Robin's not a beggar,
And Jenny Wren's a bride,
And larks hang, singing, singing, singing,
Over the wheat fields wide,
And anchored lilies ride,
And the pendulum spider
Swings from side to side,

And the blue-black beetles transact business,
And gnats fly in a host,
And furry caterpillars hasten
That no time be lost,
And moths grow fat and thrive,
And ladybirds arrive.

50

Before green apples blush,
Before green nuts embrown,
Why, one day in the country
Is worth a month in town—
Is worth a day and a year
Of the dusty, musty, lag-last fashion
That days drone elsewhere.

—*Christina Rossetti*

DO YOU FEAR THE WIND?

Do you fear the force of the wind,
The slash of the rain?
Go face them and fight them,
Be savage again.
Go hungry and cold like the wolf,
Go wade like the crane:
The palms of your hands will thicken,
The skin of your cheeks will tan,
You'll grow ragged and weary and swarthy,
But you'll walk like a man!

—*Hamlin Garland*

I Am Merchant Frost

THE MERCHANTS

I am the Frost.

I'll show you diamonds, laces, and tapestries

Of all variety,

At lowest cost;

Weavings of chaste design,

Perfect in every line;

Connoisseurs surely will buy the Frost.

52

I am the Dew.
Notice my elegant bracelets and necklaces,
All of rare quality;
Pearls not a few;
Emeralds and amethyst;
Opals all rainbow kissed;
Ladies rise early to buy of the Dew.

I am the Snow.
Let me display for you carpets most exquisite.
Choicest of bordering
Also I show,
Heavy and soft and white,
Spread in a single night;
Folks who have wisdom will buy of the Snow.

I am the Rain.
Something I'll show you priceless and wonderful
Making these offers seem
Tawdry and vain!
'Tis but a cloak of gray,
Wrapping the world away—
Happy the few who will buy of the Rain.

—*Isabell E. Mackay*

MINE HOST OF "THE GOLDEN APPLE"

A goodly host one day was mine,
A Golden Apple his only sign,
That hung from a long branch, ripe and fine.

My host was the bountiful apple tree;
He gave me shelter and nourished me
With the best of fare, all fresh and free.

And light-winged guests came not a few,
To his leafy inn, and sipped the dew,
And sang their best songs ere they flew.

I slept at night on a downy bed
Of moss, and my host benignly spread
His own cool shadow over my head.

When I asked what reckoning there might be,
He shook his broad boughs cheerily:—
A blessing be thine, green Apple tree!

—Thomas Westwood

A PRAYER

Teach me, Father, how to go
Softly as the grasses grow;
Hush my soul to meet the shock
Of the wild world as a rock;
But my spirit, propt with power,
Make as simple as a flower.
Let the dry heart fill its cup,
Like a poppy looking up;
Let life lightly wear her crown,
Like a poppy looking down.

Teach me, Father, how to be
Kind and patient as a tree.
Joyfully the crickets croon
Under shady oak at noon;
Beetle, on his mission bent,
Tarries in that cooling tent.
Let me, also, cheer a nook,
Place for friendly bread and book—
Place where passing souls can rest
On the way to be their best.

—*Edwin Markham*

OUT IN THE FIELDS WITH GOD

The little cares that fretted me
I lost them yesterday
Among the fields, above the sea,
Among the winds at play,
Among the lowing of the herds,
The rustling of the trees,
Among the singing of the birds,
The humming of the bees.

The foolish fears of what might happen,
I cast them all away,
Among the clover-scented grass,
Among the new-mown hay,
Among the husking of the corn,
Where drowsy poppies nod,
Where ill thoughts die and good are born—
Out in the fields with God.

—Elizabeth Barrett Browning

THE FAIRY FOLK

I cannot see fairies, I dream them.
There is no fairy can hide from me;
I keep on dreaming till I find him;
There you are, Primrose!
I see you, Black Wing!

—Hilda Conkling

GARDEN FAIRIES

The garden's full of fairies;
They have a happy time,
Up, up the strings of glories
They climb and climb and climb.

And then in ones, and couples,
And three, and four, and five,
As if the air were water,
They gayly dip and dive.

They climb the stalks of roses,
And hide in hollyhocks;
They play tag 'round the larkspur,
And teeter on the phlox.

The garden's full of fairies;
They dance and sing and cheer.
But when you're in the garden,
They all just disappear.

—Author Unknown

59

Sitting On a Dragon-Fly

VISION

I've seen her, I've seen her
Beneath an apple tree;
The minute that I saw her there
With stars and dewdrops in her hair,
I knew it must be she.
She's sitting on a dragon-fly
All shining green and gold,
A little way above the ground;
The dragon-fly goes circling round—
She isn't taking hold.

I've seen her, I've seen her—
I never, never knew
That anything could be so sweet;
She has the tiniest hands and feet,
Her wings are very blue.
She holds her little head like this,
Because she is a queen;
(I can't describe it all in words)
She's throwing kisses to the birds
And laughing in between.

I've seen her, I've seen her—
I simply ran and ran;
Put down your sewing quickly, please,
Let's hurry to the orchard trees
As softly as we can.
I had to go and leave her there,
I felt I couldn't stay,—
I wanted you to see her, too—
But, oh, whatever shall we do
If she has flown away?

—*Rose Fyleman*

61

THE DOOR AT THE END OF OUR GARDEN

There's a door at the end of our garden,
Covered with dust and weeds,
The key is lost and the door is locked,
And I don't know where it leads.
But every day I go there
When shadows roll in from sea,
And a dear little gold-haired Fairy
Comes through the door to me.

She tells me such lovely stories
That nobody seems to know,
Of mountains and seas and caverns
Where some day I may go;
Stories of beautiful ladies
And knights in armour of gold,
And all the wonderful gallant deeds
They did in the days of old.

I never doubt what she tells me,
I listen and long for more,
I never ask where she comes from,
Or how she gets through the door.
But *you* don't believe what I tell you,
And that very well may be,
For *you* have not seen the Fairy
Who comes through the door to me!

—*Fred E. Weatherly*

62

THE FAIRIES HAVE NEVER A PENNY
TO SPEND

The fairies have never a penny to spend,
   They haven't a thing put by;
But theirs is the dower of bird and flower,
   And theirs are the earth and the sky.
And though you should live in a palace of gold
   Or sleep in a dried-up ditch,
You could never be poor as the fairies are,
   And never as rich.

Since ever and ever the world began
   They have danced like a ribbon of flame,
They have sung their song through the centuries long,
   And yet it is never the same.
And though you be foolish, or though you be wise,
   With hair of silver or gold,
You could never be young as the fairies are,
   And never as old.

—*Rose Fyleman*

A Fairy May Be Near You

ONCE WHEN YOU WERE WALKING

Once when you were walking across the meadow grass,
A little fairy touched you—but you never saw her
pass.

One day when you were sitting upon a mossy stone,
A fairy sat beside you, but you thought you were
alone.

So no matter what you do, no matter where you go,
A fairy may be near you—but you may never know.

—Annette Wynne

FOR GOOD LUCK

Little Kings and Queens of May,
If you want to be,
Every one of you, very good,
In this beautiful, beautiful, beautiful wood,
Where the little birds' heads get so turned with delight
That some of them sing all night:
Whatever you pluck,
Leave some for good luck!

Picked from the stalk or pulled by the root,
From overhead or under foot,
Water-wonders of pond or brook—
Wherever you look,
And whatever you find,
Leave something behind:
Some for the Naiads,
Some for the Dryads,
And a bit for the Nixies and Pixies!

—Juliana Horatia Ewing

THE FAIRY QUEEN

Come follow, follow me,
You fairy elves that be:
Which circle on the green,
Come follow Mab your queen.
Hand in hand let's dance around,
For this place is fairy ground.

Upon a mushroom's head
Our table-cloth we spread.
A grain of rye or wheat
Is manchet which we eat.
Pearly drops of dew we drink
In acorn-cups filled to the brink.

The grasshopper, gnat, and fly
Serve for our minstrelsy.
Grace said, we dance awhile,
And so the time beguile.
And if the moon doth hide her head.
The glow-worm lights us home to bed.

On tops of dewy grass
So nimbly do we pass,
The young and tender stalk
Ne'er bends as we do walk;

Yet in the morning may be seen
Where we the night before have been.

—From Percy's "Reliques"

THE CHILD AND THE FAIRIES

The woods are full of fairies!
The trees are all alive:
The river overflows with them,
See how they dip and dive!
What funny little fellows!
What dainty little dears!
They dance and leap, and prance and peep,
And utter fairy cheers!

I'd like to tame a fairy,
To keep it on a shelf,
To see it wash its little face,
And dress its little self.
I'd teach it pretty manners,
It always should say "Please:"
And then you know I'd make it sew,
And curtsey with its knees!

—"A."

The Little Men

THE FAIRY FOLK

Up the airy mountain,
Down the rushy glen,
We daren't go a-hunting
For fear of little men;
Wee folk, good folk,
Trooping all together;
Green jacket, red cap,
And white owl's feather!

Down along the rocky shore
Some make their home,
They live on crispy pancakes
Of yellow tide-foam;
Some in the reeds

Of the black mountain-lake,
With frogs for their watch-dogs,
All night awake.

. . . . . .

By the craggy hill-side,
Through the mosses bare,
They have planted thorn-trees
For pleasure here and there.
Is any man so daring
As dig them up in spite?
He shall find their sharpest thorns
In his bed at night.

. . . . . .

Up the airy mountain,
Down the rushy glen,
We daren't go a-hunting
For fear of little men;
Wee folk, good folk,
Trooping all together;
Green jacket, red cap,
And white owl's feather.

—*William Allingham*

MR. MOON

A Song of the Little People

O Moon, Mr. Moon,
When you comin' down?
Down on the hilltop,
Down in the glen,
Out in the clearin',
To play with little men?
Moon, Mr. Moon,
When you comin' down?

.   .   .   .   .   .

O Mr. Moon,
Hurry up along!
The reeds in the current
Are whisperin' slow;
The river's a-wimplin'
To and fro.
Hurry up along,
Or you'll miss the song!
Moon, Mr. Moon,
When you comin' down?

.   .   .   .   .   .

O Moon, Mr. Moon,
When you comin' down?
Down where the Good Folk
Dance in a ring,
Down where the Little Folk
Sing?
Moon, Mr. Moon,
When you comin' down?

—Bliss Carman

I'D LOVE TO BE A FAIRY'S CHILD

Children born of fairy stock
Never need for shirt or frock,
Never want for food or fire,
Always get their heart's desire:
Jingle pockets full of gold,
Marry when they're seven years old.
Every fairy child may keep
Two strong ponies and ten sheep;
All have houses, each his own,
Built of brick or granite stone;
They live on cherries, they run wild—
I'd love to be a fairy's child.

—Robert Graves

71

WHERE DO FAIRIES HIDE THEIR HEADS?

Oh! where do fairies hide their heads,
When snow lies on the hills,
When frost has spoiled their mossy beds,
And crystallized their rills?
Beneath the moon they cannot trip
In circles o'er the plain;
And draughts of dew they cannot sip,
Till green leaves come again.

Perhaps, in small, blue diving-bells
They plunge beneath the waves,
Inhabiting the wreathéd shells
That lie in coral caves.
Perhaps, in red Vesuvius
Carousals they maintain;
And cheer their little spirits thus,
Till green leaves come again.

When they return, there will be mirth
And music in the air.
And fairy wings upon the earth.
And mischief everywhere.
The maids, to keep the elves aloof,
Will bar the doors in vain;
No key-hole will be fairy-proof,
When green leaves come again.

—*Thomas Haynes Bayly*

72

A-FOOT AND A-WING

All along the backwater,
Through the rushes tall,
Ducks are a-dabbling,
Up tails all!

—Kenneth Grahame

DUCKS' DITTY

All along the backwater,
Through the rushes tall,
Ducks are a-dabbling,
Up tails all!

Ducks' tails, drakes' tails,
Yellow feet a-quiver,
Yellow bills all out of sight
Busy in the river!

Slushy green undergrowth
Where the roach swim—
Here we keep our larder
Cool and full and dim!

Every one for what he likes!
We like to be
Heads down, tails up
Dabbling free!

High in the blue above
Swifts whirl and call—
We are down a-dabbling
Up tails all!

—Kenneth Grahame

75

SIR ROBIN

Rollicking Robin is here again,
What does he care for the April rain?
Care for it? Glad of it. Doesn't he know
That April rain carries off the snow,
And coaxes out leaves to shadow his nest,
And washes his pretty, red Easter vest,
And makes the juice of the cherry sweet,
For his hungry little robins to eat?
   "Ha! ha! ha!" hear the jolly bird laugh.
   "That isn't the best of the story, by half!"

Gentleman Robin, he walks up and down,
Dressed in orange-tawney and black and brown.
Though his eye is so proud and his step so firm,
He can always stoop to pick up a worm.
With a twist of his head, and a strut and a hop,
To his Robin-wife, in the peach-tree top,
Chirping her heart out, he calls: "My dear,
You don't earn your living! Come here! Come here!
   Ha! ha! ha! Life is lovely and sweet;
   But what would it be if we'd nothing to eat?"

Robin, Sir Robin, gay, red-vested knight,
Now you have come to us, summer's in sight.
You never dream of the wonders you bring,—
Visions that follow the flash of your wing.

How all the beautiful By-and-By
Around you and after you seems to fly.
Sing or eat on, as pleases your mind!
Well have you earned every morsel you find.
"Aye! Ha! ha! ha!" whistles Robin. "My dear,
Let us all take our own choice of good cheer!"

—*Lucy Larcom*

THE BLACKBIRD

In the far corner
close by the swings,
every morning
a blackbird sings.

His bill's so yellow,
his coat's so black,
that he makes a fellow
whistle back.

Ann, my daughter,
thinks that he
sings for us two
especially.

—*Humbert Wolfe*

THE BLUEBIRD

I know the song that the bluebird is singing,
Up in the apple tree where he is swinging.
Brave little fellow! the skies may be dreary,
Nothing cares he while his heart is so cheery.

Hark! how the music leaps out from his throat!
Hark! was there ever so merry a note?
Listen awhile, and you'll hear what he's saying,
Up in the apple tree, swinging and swaying:

"Dear little blossoms, down under the snow,
You must be weary of winter, I know;
Hark! while I sing you a message of cheer,
Summer is coming, and springtime is here!
Little white snowdrop, I pray you arise;
Bright yellow crocus, come, open your eyes;
Sweet little violets, hid from the cold,
Put on your mantles of purple and gold!
Daffodils, daffodils! say, do you hear?
Summer is coming, and springtime is here!"

—*Emily Huntington Miller*

HUMMING-BIRD

Why do you stand on the air

And no sun shining?

How can you hold yourself so still

On raindrops sliding?

They change and fall, they are not steady,

But you do not know they are gone.

Is there a silver wire

I cannot see?

Is the wind your perch?

Raindrops slide down your little shoulders . . .

They do not wet you.

I think you are not real

In your green feathers!

You are not a humming-bird at all

Standing on air above the garden!

I dreamed you the way I dream fairies,

Or the flower I lost yesterday!

—*Hilda Conkling*
(Written at nine years of age)

Grandmother Spider and Grasshopper Green

GRASSHOPPER GREEN

Grasshopper Green is a comical chap;
He lives on the best of fare.
Bright little trousers, jacket and cap,
These are his summer wear.
Out in the meadow he loves to go,
Playing away in the sun;
It's hopperty, skipperty, high and low—
Summer's the time for fun.

Grasshopper Green has a dozen wee boys,
And soon as their legs grow strong,
Each of them joins in his frolicsome joys,
Singing his merry song.
Under the hedge in a happy row
Soon as the day has begun,
It's hopperty, skipperty, high and low—
Summer's the time for fun.

Grasshopper Green has a quaint little house.
It's under the hedge so gay.
Grandmother Spider, as still as a mouse,
Watches him over the way.
Gladly he's calling the children, I know,
Out in the beautiful sun;
It's hopperty, skipperty, high and low—
Summer's the time for fun.

—*Author Unknown*

EARLY NEWS
The sparrow told it to the robin,
The robin told it to the wren,
Who passed it on, with sweet remark,
To thrush and bobolink and lark,
The news that dawn had come again.

—*Anna M. Pratt*

81

TO A TUFTED TITMOUSE

Ho, little bird with the crest and air
Of knowing the secrets of everywhere,
Upside down in the tall fir-tree,
Picking and pecking with rollicking glee.
Are you a bird or a fairy, say?
Or a prince bewitched for a year and a day?
Or is there shining beneath the bark,
A golden keyhole in the dark,
And a stair, where lit by the damp wood's fire,
We might climb to the Land of Heart's Desire?
Ho, little bird, your secrets tell.
Tiny gray mischief, we love you well.

—Mary Elizabeth Rodhouse

THE LILAC

Who thought of the lilac?
"I," dew said,
"I made up the lilac
out of my head."

"She made up the lilac!
Pooh!" trilled the linnet,
and each dew-note had a
lilac in it.

—Humbert Wolfe

DUCKS

When first the grass grows green in spring,
And from bare boughs the robins sing,
Before the orioles come back,
I hear the ducks go, *"Quack! quack quack!"*

They paddle round and dive and float.
Just where I like to sail my boat,
And when I run from school set free,
They make such funny eyes at me.

They never cry, nor fuss, nor fret
About the springtime rain and wet,
And have no need of sheltering roofs
Because they all wear "waterproofs."

—*Clinton Scollard*

THE SWALLOWS

Gallant and gay in their doublets gray,
All at a flash, like the darting of flame,
Chattering Arabic, African, Indian—
Certain of springtime, the swallows came!

Doublets of gray silk and surcoats of purple,
And ruffs of russet round each little throat;
Wearing such garb they had crossed the waters,
Mariners sailing with never a boat.

—*Edwin Arnold*

83

MORAL SONG

Oh, so cool
In his deep green pool
Was a frog on a log one day!
He would blink his eyes
As he snapped at flies,
   For his mother was away,
      For his mother was away!

Now that naughty frog
Left his own home log
And started out to play.
He flipped and he flopped
And he never stopped
   Till he reached the great blue bay,
      Till he reached the great blue bay!

Alas, with a swish
Came a mighty fish,
And swallowed him where he lay.
Now it's things like this
That never miss
   Little frogs who don't obey,
      Little frogs who don't obey!

                        —*John Farrar*

THE SONG OF THE CRICKET

Under the grass, in the bright summer weather,
We little crickets live gayly together;
When the moon shines, and the dew brightly glistens,
All the night long you may hear if you listen—
Cheep! Cheep! Cheep!
We are the crickets that sing you to sleep.

We have no houses to store up our treasure.
Gay little minstrels, we live but for pleasure.
What shall we do when the summer is over,
When the keen frost nips the meadows of clover?
Cheep! Cheep! Cheep!
Under the hearthstone for shelter we creep.

Then when the firelight is dancing and glowing,
Nothing we'll care how the winter is blowing;
Down in our snug little cells we will sing you
Songs of the brightness the summer will bring you.
Cheep! Cheep! Cheep!
Summer is coming, though snows may be deep.

—Emily Huntington Miller

TREE-TOAD

Tree-toad is a small gray person
With a silver voice.
Tree-toad is a leaf-gray shadow
That sings.
Tree-toad is never seen
Unless a star squeezes through the leaves,
Or a moth looks sharply at a gray branch.
How would it be, I wonder,
To sing patiently all night,
Never thinking that people are asleep?
Raindrops and mist, starriness over the trees,
The moon, the dew, the other little singers,
Cricket . . . toad . . . leaf rustling . . .
They would listen:
It would be music like weather
That gets into all the corners
Of out-of-doors.

Every night I see little shadows
I never saw before.
Every night I hear little voices
I never heard before.
When night comes trailing her starry cloak,
I start out for slumberland,
With tree-toads calling along the roadside.

Good-night, I say to one, Good-by, I say to another.
I hope to find you on the way
We have traveled before!
I hope to hear you singing on the Road of Dreams!

—Hilda Conkling
(Written at six years of age)

THE TIRED CATERPILLAR

A tired caterpillar went to sleep one day
In a snug little cradle of silken gray.
And he said, as he softly curled up in his nest,
"Oh, crawling was pleasant, but rest is best."

He slept through the winter long and cold,
All tightly up in his blanket rolled,
And at last he awoke on a warm spring day
To find that winter had gone away.

He awoke to find he had golden wings,
And no longer need crawl over sticks and things.
"Oh, the earth is nice," said the glad butterfly,
"But the sky is best, when we learn to fly!"

—Author Unknown

Cackle-cackle! Cock-a-doodle-doo!

THE FOWLS

Black hens, white hens, speckled hens and brown,
Clucking in the sunshine, strutting up and down;
Very vain and happy they, for were the truth but
    known,
Each thinks the loudest cackle in the farm-yard is her
    own,
And each declares the egg she's left behind her in the
    nest
Is bigger and much better than the eggs of all the rest.

    "Cackle-cackle! Cluck-a-cluck!
    Cock-a-doodle-doo!
    The Cock is king of Farm-yard Land,
    But I am queen there too."

88

White hens, brown hens, speckled hens and black,
With lots of little chicks a-toddling at their back;
Father Cock must come and look, his red comb on his
    head.
Cheep at him, my pretties! Sir, be careful how you
    tread!
Now are they not a lovely brood? Just see them peck
    and run;
And see how my two soft warm wings will cover every
    one.

"Cackle-cackle! Cheepie-cheep!
Ah, cock-a-doodle-doo;
Although you're king of Farm-yard Land
I'm prouder far than you!"

—*Madeleine Nightingale*

HONEY-BEE

Honey-bee, honey-bee! here is some money;
Take it and bring us a pot of new honey!
Fly away! fly, you buzzing old rover!
Gather us sweets from the blossoming clover.

—*Lucy Fitch Perkins*

THE SONG OF THE BEE

Buzz! buzz! buzz!
This is the song of the bee.
His legs are of yellow;
A jolly, good fellow,
And yet a great worker is he.

In days that are sunny
He's getting his honey.
In days that are cloudy
He's making his wax.
On pinks and on lilies,
And gay daffodillies,
And columbine blossoms
He levies his tax.

Buzz! buzz! buzz!
The sweet-smelling clover,
He, humming, hangs over.
The scent of the roses
Makes fragrant his wings.
He never gets lazy.
From thistle and daisy,
And weeds of the meadow,
Some treasure he brings.

Buzz! buzz! buzz!
From morning's first light
Till the coming of night,
He's singing and toiling
The summer day through.
Oh! we may get weary,
And think work is dreary.
'Tis harder by far
To have nothing to do.

—*Marian Douglas*

THE HAPPY SHEEP

All through the night the happy sheep
Lie in the meadow grass asleep.

Their wool keeps out the frost and rain
Until the sun comes round again.

They have no buttons to undo,
No hair to brush, like me and you.

And with the light they lift their heads
To find their breakfast on their beds,

Or rise and walk about and eat
The carpet underneath their feet.

—*Wilfred Thorley*

QUESTIONS

I visited the animals,
That live in our Zoo;
And there are lots of questions
I've saved to ask of you.

Why is the zebra's skin so tight?
The hippo's skin so loose?
Why does the old owl look so wise?
The peacock such a goose?

What do the monkeys talk about
In their excited way?
I'm sure it would be lots of fun
If we knew what they say!

The turtle's house is fastened on
As tight as can be!
Are little boys as queer to them
As turtles are to me?

—*Ruth Collat*

MAKE-BELIEVE

Which is the way to Somewhere Town?
Oh, up in the morning early;
Over the tiles and the chimney pots,
That is the way quite clearly.

—Kate Greenaway

MAKE-BELIEVE LAND

Ho, Little Boy Blue, come climb on my knee,
And cuddle up closely, as snug as can be;
With gently closed eyelids and lightly clasped hand
We'll journey together to Make-Believe Land.

The Genii and Fairies and Trolls of the Hill,
You'll find there a-waiting to do what you will;
Oh, a wonderful company, a right loyal band
Are these queer little people of Make-Believe Land.

They'll make all your wishes come true as can be;
They'll carry you swiftly to lands o'er the sea;
They'll change poorest homes to palaces grand,
But that's nothing strange in Make-Believe Land.

Your soldiers of tin, in their colors so gay,
Will all become real in martial array.
Then clap on your helmet! and saber in hand,
Hurrah for the armies of Make-Believe Land!

Your engine has steam up all ready to go,
The track is all clean—but be sure to go slow,
And see that your train is properly manned,
For awful wrecks happen in Make-Believe Land.

—*Eugene Field*

THE LAND OF STORY-BOOKS

At evening when the lamp is lit,
Around the fire my parents sit;
They sit at home and talk and sing,
And do not play at anything.

Now, with my little gun, I crawl
All in the dark along the wall,
And follow round the forest track
Away behind the sofa back.

There, in the night, where none can spy,
All in my hunter's camp I lie,
And play at books that I have read
Till it is time to go to bed.

These are the hills, these are the woods,
These are my starry solitudes;
And there the river by whose brink
The roaring lions come to drink.

I see the others far away
As if in firelit camp they lay,
And I, like to an Indian scout,
Around their party prowled about.

So, when my nurse comes in for me,
Home I return across the sea,
And go to bed with backward looks
At my dear land of Story-books.

—Robert Louis Stevenson

VERY LOVELY

Wouldn't it be lovely if the rain came down
Till the water was quite high over all the town?
If the cabs and busses all were set afloat,
And we had to go to school in a little boat?

Wouldn't it be lovely if it still should pour
And we all went up to live on the second floor?
If we saw the butcher sailing up the hill,
And we took the letters in at the window sill?

It's been raining, raining, all the afternoon;
All these things might happen really very soon.
If we woke to-morrow and found they had begun,
Wouldn't it be glorious? *Wouldn't* it be fun?

—Rose Fyleman

Just Like a Bright Rainbow

BLOWING BUBBLES

You hurry so each time you blow,
Of course they'll never last!
You puff them all to pieces, 'cause
You blow so hard and fast.
Blow short and softly—that's the way
To make the biggest bubbles stay.

All pink and blue and purple too,
Just like a rainbow bright,
You see how long it's lasted—

That's 'cause I blew it right.
Now one long puff, and it will fly
To join the rainbow in the sky.

—Burges Johnson

A STORMY DAY

I look out through the window where
The world is wet and wild,
And fancy I am wandering there,
A lost and dripping child.

That makes it pleasant when I turn
And find I am myself,
With food to eat and wood to burn,
And toys upon the shelf.

Or else, a shipwrecked sailor-boy,
Upon the rug I lie,
And thankfully the fire enjoy
Until my clothes are dry.

Or sometimes, when a deluge falls,
At Noah's Ark I play,
And being all the animals
Gives me a busy day.

—Mrs. Van Rensselaer

BLOCK CITY

What are you able to build with your blocks?
Castles and palaces, temples and docks.
Rain may keep raining, and others go roam,
But I can be happy and building at home.

Let the sofa be mountains, the carpet be sea,
There I'll establish a city for me:
A kirk and a mill and a palace beside,
And a harbor as well, where my vessels may ride.

Great is the palace with pillar and wall,
A sort of a tower on the top of it all,
And steps coming down in an orderly way
To where my toy vessels lie safe in the bay.

This one is sailing and that one is moored.
Hark to the song of the sailors on board!
And see, on the steps of my palace, the kings
Coming and going with presents and things!

Now I have done with it, down let it go!
All in a moment the town is laid low.
Block upon block lying scattered and free,
What is there left of my town by the sea?

Yet as I saw it, I see it again,
The kirk and the palace, the ships and the men,
And as long as I live, and where'er I may be,
I'll always remember my town by the sea.

—*Robert Louis Stevenson*

UNDERNEATH THE CLOTHES

I'm sure that no one ever knows
The fun I have beneath the clo'se.
I snuggle down inside the bed,
And cover all my face and head.

It's p'raps a coal-mine, p'raps a cave,
And sometimes, when I'm very brave,
It's Daniel's den with three or four,
Or even six real lions that roar.

It's most exciting how it goes—
The road that leads beneath the clo'se;
You never can tell how it ends,
Because, you see, it all depends.

—*Madeleine Nightingale*

DAFFODIL TIME

It is daffodil time, so the robins all cry,
For the sun's a big daffodil up in the sky,
And when down the midnight the owl calls
    "to-whoo!"
Why, then the round moon is a daffodil, too;
Now sheer to the bough-tops the sap starts to climb,
So, merry my masters, it's daffodil time!

It is time for the song; it is time for the sonnet;
It is time for Belinda to have a new bonnet,
All fashioned and furbished with things that are fair,
To rest like a crown on her daffodil hair;
Love beats in the heart like the pulse of a rhyme,
So, merry my masters, it's daffodil time!

It is time when the vales and the hills cry "Away!
Come, join in the joy of the daffodil day!"
For somewhere one waits, with a glow on her face,
With her daffodil smile and her daffodil grace.
There's a lilt in the air, there's a cheer, there's a chime,
So, merry my masters, it's daffodil time!

—Clinton Scollard

A TEA-PARTY

You see, merry Phillis, that dear little maid,
Has invited Belinda to tea;
Her nice little garden is shaded by trees,—
What pleasanter place could there be?

There's a cake full of plums, there are strawberries too,
And the table is set on the green;
I'm fond of a carpet all daisies and grass,—
Could a prettier picture be seen?

A blackbird (yes, blackbirds delight in warm
        weather,)
Is flitting from yonder high spray;
He sees the two little ones talking together;—
No wonder the blackbird is gay.

—Kate Greenaway

Gretchen in Her Garden

A LITTLE DUTCH GARDEN

I passed by a garden, a little Dutch garden,
Where useful and pretty things grew,—
Heartsease and tomatoes, and pinks and potatoes,
And lilies and onions and rue.

I saw in that garden, that little Dutch garden.
A chubby Dutch man with a spade,
And a rosy Dutch frau with a shoe like a scow,
And a flaxen-haired little Dutch maid.

There grew in that garden, that little Dutch garden,
Blue flag flowers lovely and tall,
And early blush roses, and little pink posies,
And Gretchen was fairer than all.

My heart's in that garden, that little Dutch garden,—
It tumbled right in as I passed,
'Mid wildering mazes of spinach and daisies,
And Gretchen is holding it fast.

—*Harriet Whitney Durbin*

A COMPARISON

Snow falls softly, but
Apple blossoms look like snow,
They're different, though.
Snow falls softly, but it brings
Noisy things:
Sleighs and bells, forts and fights,
Cosy nights.

But apple blossoms when they go,
White and slow,
Quiet all the orchard space,
Till the place
Hushed with falling sweetness seems
Filled with dreams.

—*John Farrar*

ONE, TWO, THREE

It was an old, old, old, old lady,
And a boy that was half-past three;
And the way that they played together
Was beautiful to see.

She couldn't go romping and jumping,
And the boy no more could he;
For he was a thin little fellow,
With a thin little twisted knee.

They sat in the yellow sunlight,
Out under the maple tree;
And the game they played I'll tell you,
Just as it was told to me.

It was Hide-and-Go-Seek they were playing,
Though you'd never have known it to be—
With an old, old, old, old lady,
And a boy with a twisted knee.

The boy would bend his face down
On his little sound right knee,
And he guessed where she was hiding
In guesses One, Two, Three.

"You are in the china closet!"
He would laugh and cry with glee—
It wasn't the china closet,
But he still had Two and Three.

"You are up in papa's big bedroom,
In the chest with the queer old key!"
And she said: "You are *warm* and *warmer;*
But you are not quite right," said she.

"It can't be the little cupboard
Where mama's things used to be—
So it must be in the clothes-press, Gran'ma,"
And he found her with his Three.

Then she covered her face with her fingers,
That were wrinkled and white and wee,
And she guessed where the boy was hiding,
With a One and a Two and a Three.

And they never had stirred from their places
Right under the maple tree—
This old, old, old, old lady
And the boy with the lame little knee—
This dear, dear, dear old lady,
And the boy who was half-past three.

—Henry Cuyler Bunner

THE SUGAR-PLUM TREE

Have you ever heard of the Sugar-Plum Tree?
'Tis a marvel of great renown!
It blooms on the shore of the Lollypop sea
In the garden of Shut-Eye Town;
The fruit that it bears is so wondrously sweet
(As those who have tasted it say)
That good little children have only to eat
Of that fruit to be happy next day.

When you've got to the tree, you would have a hard
    time
To capture the fruit which I sing;
The tree is so tall that no person could climb
To the boughs where the sugar-plums swing!
But up in that tree sits a chocolate cat,
And a gingerbread dog prowls below—
And this is the way you contrive to get at
    Those sugar-plums tempting you so:

You say but the word to that gingerbread dog
And he barks with such terrible zest
That the chocolate cat is at once all agog,
As her swelling proportions attest.

And the chocolate cat goes cavorting around
From this leafy limb unto that,
And the sugar-plums tumble, of course, to the
    ground—
Hurrah for that chocolate cat!

There are marshmallows, gumdrops, and peppermint
    canes
With stripings of scarlet or gold,
And you carry away of the treasure that rains,
As much as your apron can hold!
So come, little child, cuddle closer to me
In your dainty white nightcap and gown,
And I'll rock you away to that Sugar-Plum Tree
In the garden of Shut-Eye Town.

—*Eugene Field*

A CHRISTMAS WISH

I'd like a stocking made for a giant,
And a meeting house full of toys,
Then I'd go out in a happy hunt
For the poor little girls and boys;
Up the street and down the street,
And across and over the town,
I'd search and find them every one,
Before the sun went down.

One would want a new jack-knife
Sharp enough to cut;
One would long for a doll with hair,
And eyes that open and shut;
One would ask for a china set
With dishes all to her mind;
One would wish a Noah's ark
With beasts of every kind.

Some would like a doll's cook-stove
And a little toy wash tub;
Some would prefer a little drum,
For a noisy rub-a-dub;

Some would wish for a story book,
And some for a set of blocks;
Some would be wild with happiness
Over a new tool-box.

And some would rather have little shoes,
And other things warm to wear;
For many children are very poor
And the winter is hard to bear;
I'd buy soft flannels for little frocks,
And a thousand stockings or so,
And the jolliest little coats and cloaks
To keep out the frost and snow.

I'd load a wagon with caramels
And candy of every kind,
And buy all the almond and pecan nuts
And taffy that I could find;
And barrels and barrels of oranges
I'd scatter right in the way,
So the children would find them the
       very first thing
When they wake on Christmas day.

—*Eugene Field*

Cinderella Meets Her Prince

AFTER ALL AND AFTER ALL

Dreaming of a prince
Cinderella sat among the ashes long ago;
Dreaming of a prince,
She scoured the pots and kettles till they shone: and so,
After all and after all,
Gaily at the castle ball
Cinderella met her prince long and long ago.

Dreaming of a prince,
Sleeping Beauty lay in happy slumber, white and
    still;
Dreaming of a prince,
She waited for a hundred years, and then his bugles
    shrill,

After all and after all,
Woke the castle, bower, and hall,
And he found her waiting for him long and long ago.

Dreaming of a prince
I polish bowl and teapot and the spoons, each one;
Dreaming of a prince,
I hang the new-washed clothes to wave a-drying in the
    sun;
After all and after all,
Great adventures may befall
Like to those that happened once long and long ago.

—*Mary Carolyn Davies*

MAKE-BELIEVE TOWN

Oh, Make-Believe Town is a place of delight,
Where wondrous things happen from morning till
    night.
You may go there in tatters, when, lo! and behold!
In an instant you're decked out in velvet and gold.

You take there a broomstick, and, quick as a flash,
It's transformed to a charger, all fire and dash!
Or a lovely white pony with long, silky mane,
Side-saddle, gilt stirrups, and blue-ribbon rein!

113

The old rocking-chair, without arms or a back,
Can be changed to a chariot, engine, or hack.
The plain wooden floor in five minutes can be
A race-course, a circus, a desert, a sea!

And the closet, a castle where big giants wait
To capture the first one who comes to their gate!
In a wink it's a cave where bold robbers hide,
Or a den where fierce dragons and ogres abide!

You've only to wish it, when lo! at your feet
Is a fine desert island, rock-bound and complete!
You've only to speak—in an instant you can
Be Robinson Crusoe, or Friday, his man!

Whatever you wish for, it's waiting for you;
Whatever you dream of, that dream will come true!
You can be what you will, from a king to a clown,
If once you gain entrance to Make-Believe Town.

—Claudia Tharin

114

JUST FOR FUN

There was an old man with a beard,
Who said, "It is just as I feared!—
Two owls and a hen, four larks and a wren
Have all built their nests in my beard."

— Edward Lear

THE FUNNIEST THING IN THE WORLD

The funniest thing in the world, I know,
Is watchin' the monkeys 'at's in the show!—
Jumpin' an' runnin' an' racin' roun',
'Way up the top o' the pole, nen down!
First they're here, an' nen they're there,
An' ist a'most any an' ever'where!—
Screechin' an' scratchin' wherever they go,
They're the funniest thing in the world, I know!

They're the funniest thing in the world, I think:—
Funny to watch 'em eat an' drink;
Funny to watch 'em a-watchin' us,
An' actin' 'most like grown folks does!—
Funny to watch 'em p'tend to be
Skeerd at their tail 'at they happen to see;—
But the funniest thing in the world they do
Is never to laugh, like me an' you!

—*James Whitcomb Riley*

THE DUEL

The gingham dog and the calico cat
Side by side on the table sat;
'Twas half-past twelve, and (what do you think!)
Nor one nor t'other had slept a wink!
The old Dutch clock and the Chinese plate
Appeared to know as sure as fate
There was going to be a terrible spat.
(I wasn't there; I simply state
What was told to me by the Chinese plate!)

The gingham dog went "bow-wow-wow!"
And the calico cat replied "mee-ow!"
The air was littered, an hour or so,
With bits of gingham and calico,
While the old Dutch clock in the chimney-place
Up with its hands before its face,
For it always dreaded a family row!
(Now mind: I'm only telling you
What the old Dutch clock declares is true!)

The Chinese plate looked very blue.

And wailed, "Oh, dear! what shall we do!"

But the gingham dog and the calico cat

Wallowed this way and tumbled that,

Employing every tooth and claw

In the awfullest way you ever saw—

And, oh! how the gingham and calico flew!

(Don't fancy I exaggerate!

I got my news from the Chinese plate!)

Next morning where the two had sat,

They found no trace of dog or cat;

And some folks think unto this day

That burglars stole that pair away!

But the truth about the cat and pup

Is this: they ate each other up!

Now what do you really think of that!

(The old Dutch clock it told me so,

And that is how I came to know.)

—*Eugene Field*

119

THE BOY WITH THE LITTLE BARE TOES

He ran all down the meadow, that he did,
The boy with the little bare toes.
The flowers they smelt so sweet, so sweet,
And the grass it felt so funny and wet
And the birds sang just like this—"chereep!"
And the willow-trees stood in rows.
"Ho! ho!"
Laughed the boy with the little bare toes.

Now the trees had no insides—"How funny!"
Laughed the boy with the little bare toes.
And he put in his hand to find some money
Or honey—yes, that would be best—oh, best!
But what do you think he found, found, found?
Why, six little eggs all round, round, round,
And a mother-bird on the nest,
Oh, yes!
The mother-bird on her nest.

He laughed, "Ha! ha!" and he laughed, "He! he!"
The boy with the little bare toes.
But the little mother-bird got up from her place
And flew right into his face, "Ho! ho!"
And pecked him on the nose, "Oh! oh!"

Yes, pecked him right on the nose.
"Boo! hoo!"
Cried the boy with the little bare toes.

—*William Harvey*

———

THE WREN AND THE HEN

Said a very small wren
To a very large hen:
"Pray, why do you make such a clatter?
I never could guess
Why an egg, more or less,
Should be thought so important a matter."

Then answered the hen
To the very small wren:
"If I laid such small eggs as you, madam,
I would not cluck loud,
Nor would I feel proud.
Look at these! How you'd crow, if you had 'em!"

—*Author Unknown*

"Ker-chunk!   Ker-chunk!"

THE FROGS' SINGING SCHOOL

Down in the rushes beside the pool,
The frogs were having a singing-school;
Old frogs, young frogs, tadpoles and all,
Doing their best at their leader's call.
He waved a grass-blade high in the air,
And cried, "Ker-chunk!" which means "Prepare!"
But the youngest singer took up the strain,
And sang, "Ker-chunk!" with might and main.
The others followed as he sang;
"Ker-chunk!" their voices loudly rang.
Until their leader so angry grew
He snapped his baton quite in two,
And croaked, "Oh, wrong; oh, wro-ong!
        oh, wro-ong!"

Which his class mistook for another song.
At that, their leader hopped away—
"Ker-chunk! oh, wro-ong!" I heard him say.
Then flop! he went, right into the pool.
And that was the end of the singing-school.

—E. T. Corbell

THE YAK

As a friend to the children commend me the Yak.
You will find it exactly the thing;
It will carry and fetch, you can ride on its back,
Or lead it about with a string.

The Tartar who dwells on the plains of Thibet
(A desolate region of snow)
Has for centuries made it a nursery pet,
And surely the Tartar should know!

Then tell your papa where the Yak can be got,
And if he is awfully rich,
He will buy you the creature—or else he will not.
(I cannot be positive which.)

—Hilaire Belloc

123

GUESSING SONG

Oh ho! oh ho! Pray, who can I be?
I sweep o'er the land, I scour o'er the sea;
I cuff the tall trees till they bow down their heads,
And I rock the wee birdies asleep in their beds.
Oh ho! oh ho! And who can I be,
That sweep o'er the land and scour o'er the sea?

I rumple the breast of the gray-headed daw,
I tip the rook's tail up and make him cry "caw":
But though I love fun, I'm so big and so strong,
At a puff of my breath the great ships sail along.
Oh ho! oh ho! And who can I be,
That sweep o'er the land and sail o'er the sea?

I swing all the weather-cocks this way and that.
I play hare-and-hounds with a runaway hat;
But however I wander, I never can stray,
For go where I will, I've a free right of way!
Oh ho! oh ho! And who can I be,
That sweep o'er the land and scour o'er the sea?

I skim o'er the heather, I dance up the street,
I've foes that I laugh at, and friends that I greet;
I'm known in the country, I'm named in the town,
For all the world over extends my renown.
Oh ho! oh ho! And who can I be,
That sweep o'er the land and scour o'er the sea?

—*Henry Johnstone*

THE MAN IN THE MOON

The Man in the Moon as he sails the sky
Is a very remarkable skipper,
But he made a mistake when he tried to take
A drink of milk from the Dipper.
He dipped right out of the Milky Way,
And slowly and carefully filled it,
The Big Bear growled, and the Little Bear howled
And frightened him so that he spilled it!

—*Old Rhyme*

THE LOOKING-GLASS WORLD

To the Looking-Glass world it was Alice that said,
"I've a sceptre in hand, I've a crown on my head,
Let the Looking-Glass creatures, whatever they be,
Come and dine with the Red Queen, the White Queen,
    and me!"

Then fill up the glasses as quick as you can,
And sprinkle the table with buttons and bran;
Put cats in the coffee, and mice in the tea—
And welcome Queen Alice with thirty-times-three!

"O Looking-Glass creatures," quoth Alice, "draw
    near!
'Tis an honor to see me, a favor to hear;
'Tis a privilege high to have dinner and tea
Along with the Red Queen, the White Queen, and
    me!"

Then fill up the glasses with treacle and ink,
Or anything else that is pleasant to drink;
Mix sand with the cider, and wool with the wine—
And welcome Queen Alice with ninety-times-nine!

—*Lewis Carroll*

THE ELF AND THE DORMOUSE

Under a toadstool crept a wee Elf,
Out of the rain, to shelter himself.

Under a toadstool sound asleep,
Sat a big Dormouse all in a heap.

Trembled the wee Elf, frightened, and yet
Fearing to fly away lest he get wet.

To the next shelter—maybe a mile!
Sudden the wee Elf smiled a wee smile,

Tugged till the toadstool toppled in two.
Holding it over him, gayly he flew.

Soon he was safe home, dry as could be.
Soon woke the Dormouse—"Good gracious me!

"Where is my toadstool?" loud he lamented,
And that's how umbrellas first were invented.

—Oliver Herford

If the butterfly courted the bee,
And the owl the porcupine;
If churches were built in the sea,
And three times one was nine;
If the pony rode his master,
If the buttercups ate the cows,
If the cats had the dire disaster
To be worried, sir, by the mouse;
If Mamma, sir, sold the baby
To a gypsy for half a crown;
If a gentleman, sir, was a lady,—
The world would be Upside-down!
If any or all of these wonders
Should ever come about,
I should not consider them blunders,
For I should be Inside-out!

Chorus

Ba-ba, black wool,
Have you any sheep?
Yes, sir a packfull,
Creep, mouse, creep!

Four-and-twenty little maids
Hanging out the pie,
Out jumped the honey-pot,
Guy Fawkes, Guy!
Cross latch, cross latch,
Sit and spin the fire;
When the pie was opened,
The bird was on the brier!

—*William Brighty Rands*

THE PUZZLED CENTIPEDE

A centipede was happy quite,
Until a frog in fun
Said, "Pray, which leg comes after which?"
This raised her mind to such a pitch,
She lay distracted in the ditch
Considering how to run.

—*Author Unknown*

THREE WISE OLD WOMEN

Three wise old women were they, were they,

Who went to walk on a winter day.

One carried a basket to hold some berries,

One carried a ladder to climb for cherries,

The third, and she was the wisest one,

Carried a fan to keep off the sun!

But they went so far, and they went so fast,

They quite forgot their way at last—

So one of the wise women cried in fright,

"Suppose we should meet a bear tonight!

Suppose he should eat me!"
                    "And me!!"
                         "And me!!!"
"What is to be done?" cried all the three.

"Dear, dear!" said one, "we'll climb a tree;

Then out of the way of the bears we'll be."

But there wasn't a tree for miles around;

They were too frightened to stay on the ground;

So they climbed their ladder up to the top,

And sat there screaming, "We'll drop, we'll drop!"

But the wind was strong as wind could be,

And blew their ladder right out to sea!

So the three wise women were all afloat

In a leaky ladder instead of a boat;

And every time the waves rolled in,

Of course the poor things were wet to the skin.

Then they took their basket the water to bail,

They put up their fan instead of a sail;

But what became of the wise women then—

Whether they ever sailed home again—

Whether they saw any bears or no—

You must find out, for I don't know.

—*E. T. Corbell*

131

THE AMBITIOUS MOUSE

If all the world were candy
And the sky were frosted cake,
Oh, it would be a splendid job
For a mouse to undertake!

To eat a path of sweetmeats
Through candy forest aisles—
Explore the land of Pepper-mint
Stretched out for miles and miles.

To gobble up a cloudlet,
A little cup-cake star,
To swim a lake of liquid sweet
With shores of chocolate bar.

But best of all the eating
Would be the toothsome fat
Triumphant hour of mouse-desire,
To eat a candy cat!

—John Farrar

SHADOW TIME

When the shades of night are falling,
And the sun goes down,
Oh, the Dustman comes a-creeping in
From Shut-Eye Town!

—*Anonymous*

ESCAPE AT BEDTIME

The lights from the parlor and kitchen shone out
Through the blinds and the windows and bars;
And high overhead and all moving about,
There were thousands and millions of stars.

There ne'er were such thousands of leaves on a tree,
Nor of people in church or the Park,
As the crowds of the stars that looked down upon me,
And that glittered and winked in the dark.

The Dog, and the Plough, and the Hunter, and all,
And the star of the Sailor, and Mars.
These shone in the sky, and the pail by the wall
Would be half full of water and stars.

They saw me at last, and they chased me with cries,
And they soon had me packed into bed;
But the glory kept shining and bright in my eyes,
And the stars going round in my head.

—*Robert Louis Stevenson*

ANIMAL CRACKERS

Animal crackers and cocoa to drink,
That is the finest of suppers, I think;
When I'm grown up and can have what I please
I think I shall always insist upon these.

What do *you* choose when you're offered a treat?
When Mother says, "What would you like best to
        eat?"
Is it waffles and syrup, or cinnamon toast?
It's cocoa and animals that I love the most!

The kitchen's the cosiest place that I know:
The kettle is singing, the stove is aglow,
And there in the twilight, how jolly to see
The cocoa and animals waiting for me.

Daddy and Mother dine later in state,
With Mary to cook for them, Susan to wait;
But they don't have nearly as much fun as I
Who eat in the kitchen with Nurse standing by;
And Daddy once said he would like to be me
Having cocoa and animals once more for tea!

—*Christopher Morley*

THE STARS IN TOWN

At the seashore last week they showed me the stars,

And taught me the names of a few,

And the patterns they made, with their spangles of
  gold,

On a sky that was darker than blue.

When we strolled after supper to-night in the Park,

As I sometimes may do for a treat,

The very same stars—oh, I jumped with surprise—

Shone high over housetop and street.

The Dipper was there, and the zigzag-y Chair,

And the Star of the North looking down.

At the seashore, I wonder, what shines in the place

Of the stars that have moved into town?

—*Mrs. Van Rensselaer*

POPPIES

The poppies in the garden, they all wear frocks of silk,

Some are purple, some are pink, and others white as
milk,

Light, light for dancing in—for dancing when the
breeze

Plays a little two-step for the blossoms and the bees:

Fine, fine for dancing—all frilly at the hem.

Oh! when I watch the poppies dance, I long to dance
like them.

The poppies in the garden have let their silk frocks fall

All about the border paths; but where are they at all?

Here a frill, and there a flounce—a rag of silky red,

But not a poppy-girl is left; I think they've gone to
bed;

Gone to bed and gone to sleep, and weary they must
be,

For each has left her box of dreams upon the stem for
me.

—Ffrida Wolfe

138

MOON SO ROUND AND YELLOW

Moon so round and yellow,

Looking from on high,

How I love to see you

Shining in the sky.

Oft and oft I wonder,

When I see you there,

How they get to light you

Hanging in the air:

Where you go at morning,

When the night is past,

And the sun comes peeping

O'er the hills at last.

Sometime I will watch you

Slyly overhead,

When you think I'm sleeping

Snugly in my bed.

—*Matthias Barr*

MY SHADOW

I have a little shadow that goes in and out with me,
And what can be the use of him is more than I can see.
He is very, very like me from the heels up to the head;
And I see him jump before me, when I jump into my
    bed.

The funniest thing about him is the way he likes to
    grow—
Not at all like proper children, which is always very
    slow;
For he sometimes shoots up taller like an india-rubber
    ball,
And he sometimes gets so little that there's none of him
    at all.

He hasn't got a notion of how children ought to play,
And can only make a fool of me in every sort of way.
He stays so close beside me, he's a coward you can see;
I'd think shame to stick to nursie as that shadow sticks
    to me!

One morning, very early, before the sun was up,
I rose and found the shining dew on every buttercup;

But my lazy little shadow, like an arrant sleepy-head,
Had stayed at home behind me, and was fast asleep in
bed.

—Robert Louis Stevenson

SHADOW-TOWN FERRY

Sway to and fro in the twilight gray;
This is the ferry to Shadow-town.
It always sails at the end of day,
Just as the darkness is coming down.

Rest, little head, on my shoulder, so—
A sleepy kiss is the only fare;
Drifting away from the world we go,
Baby and I in the rocking chair.

See, where the fire-logs glow and spark
Glitter the lights of the shadow-land!
The winter rains on the window—hark!—
Are ripples lapping upon its strand.

Rock slow, more slow, in the dusky light,
Silently lower the anchor down.
Dear little passenger, say "Good-night!"
We have reached the harbor of Shadow-town.

—Lillian Dynevor Rice

A Silver Cradle

THE NEW MOON

Dear mother, how pretty
The moon looks to-night!
She was never so cunning before;
Her two little horns
Are so sharp and so bright,
I hope she'll not grow any more.

If I were up there,
With you and my friends,

142

I'd rock in it nicely, you'd see;

I'd sit in the middle

And hold by both ends;

Oh, what a bright cradle 'twould be!

I would call to the stars

To keep out of the way,

Lest we should rock over their toes;

And then I would rock

Till the dawn of the day,

And see where the pretty moon goes.

And there we would stay

In the beautiful skies,

And through the bright clouds we would roam;

We would see the sun set,

And see the sun rise,

And on the next rainbow come home.

—*Eliza Lee Follen*

ROCK-A-BYE

Rock-a-bye, Lilla,
Rock-a-bye—low!
Off into sleepy land Lilla must go;
For Dollies must sleep
Like the rest of the world,
So rock-a-bye, Lilla! Rock-a-bye—low!

Rock-a-bye, Lilla,
Rock-a-bye—dear,
You needn't worry, *you* needn't fear;
No powders to take,
No prayers to be said,
So rock-a-bye, dear, in your dear little bed.

Then rock-a-bye, Lilla,
Rock-a-bye—low!
What does it matter how old you may grow,
Battered or broken,
Howe'er you may be,
You are the dearest of Dollies to me!

—*Fred E. Weatherly*

WHERE DREAMS ARE MADE

Dreams are made in the moon, my dear,
On her shining hillsides steep;
Pleasant and dreadful and gay and queer,
They're piled in a silver heap.
And many fairies with buzzing wings
Are busy with hammers and wheels and things,
Making the dreams that night-time brings
To all little boys asleep.

And if a boy has been good till night,
When snug in his bed he lies,
The fairies come with a moonbeam bright
And slide him up to the skies.
And there he sails as the Moon-king's guest,
And chooses the dreams he likes the best;
Then they slide him back to his nurs'ry nest
And leave him rubbing his eyes.

—*Burges Johnson*

145

AULD DADDY DARKNESS

Auld Daddy Darkness creeps frae his hole,
Black as a blackmoor, blin' as a mole.
Stir the fire till it lowes, let the bairnie sit,
Auld Daddy Darkness is no wantit yit.

See him in the corners hidin' frae the licht,
See him at the window gloomin' at the nicht;
Turn up the gas licht, close the shutters a',
An' Auld Daddy Darkness will flee far awa'.

Awa' to hide the birdie within its cosy nest,
Awa' to lap the wee flooers on their mither's breast,
Awa' to loosen Gaffer Toil frae his daily ca',
For Auld Daddy Darkness is kindly to a'.

He comes when we're weary to wean's frae oor waes,
He comes when the bairnies are getting off their claes,
To cover them sae cosy, an' bring bonnie dreams;
So Auld Daddy Darkness is better than he seems.

Steek yer een, my wee tot, ye'll see Daddy then;
He's in below the bed claes, to cuddle ye he's fain;
Noo nestle to his bosie, sleep and dream yer fill,
Till Wee Davie Daylight comes keekin' owre the hill.

—*James Ferguson*

A CHILD'S THOUGHT OF GOD

They say that God lives very high!
But if you look above the pines
You cannot see our God. And why?

And if you dig down in the mines,
You never see Him in the gold,
Though from Him all that's glory shines.

God is so good, He wears a fold
Of heaven and earth across His face—
Like secrets kept for love untold.

But still I feel that His embrace
Slides down by thrills through all things made,
Through sight and sound of every place:

As if my tender mother laid
On my shut lids her kisses' pressure,
Half-waking me at night; and said,
"Who kissed you through the dark, dear guesser?"

—Elizabeth Barrett Browning

CHILD AND MOTHER

O Mother-My-Love, if you'll give me your hand,
And go where I ask you to wander,
I will lead you away to a beautiful land—
The Dreamland that's waiting out yonder.
We'll walk in a sweet posie-garden out there,
Where moonlight and starlight are streaming,
And the flowers and the birds are filling the air
With the fragrance and music of dreaming.

There'll be no little tired-out boy to undress,
No questions or cares to perplex you;
There'll be no little bruises or bumps to caress,
Nor patching of stocking to vex you.
For I'll rock you away on a silver-dew stream
And sing you asleep when you're weary,
And no one shall know of our beautiful dream
But you and your own little dearie.

And when I am tired I'll nestle my head
In the bosom that's soothed me so often,
And the wide-awake stars shall sing in my stead
A song which our dreaming shall soften.
So, Mother-My-Love, let me take your dear hand
And away through the starlight we'll wander—

Away through the mist to the beautiful land—
The Dreamland that's waiting out yonder!

———

THE PRAYER PERFECT

Dear Lord! Kind Lord!
Gracious Lord! I pray
Thou wilt look on all I love
Tenderly to-day;
Weed their hearts of weariness,
Scatter every care
Down a wake of angel-wings
Winnowing the air.
Bring unto the sorrowing
All release from pain;
Let the lips of laughter
Overflow again;
And with all the needy
O divide, I pray,
This vast treasure of content
That is mine to-day.

—James Whitcomb Riley

TODAY

Here hath been dawning
Another blue day;
Think, wilt thou let it
Slip useless away?

Out of Eternity
This new day was born;
Into Eternity
At night will return.

Behold it aforetime
No eye ever did;
So soon it forever
From all eyes is hid.

Here hath been dawning
Another blue day;
Think, wilt thou let it
Slip useless away?

—*Thomas Carlyle*

Good-Night!

A THOUGHT

O bird upon the bough,

Thou art God's voice to me;

O star in midnight sky,

Thou art my Father's ever watchful eye.

—*Florence Sampson*

151

ACKNOWLEDGMENTS

The editor is indebted to the following publishers and authors who have generously cooperated in the publication of this volume by granting permission to include copyright material. All rights to the poems are reserved by the legal holders of the copyrights.

THE BOBBS-MERRILL COMPANY: "The Funniest Thing in the World" and "The Prayer Perfect" from "Rhymes of Childhood" by James Whitcomb Riley, copyright 1890 to 1918.

ERNEST BENN, Ltd., London: "The Blackbird" and "The Lilac" from "The Unknown Goddess," by Humbert Wolfe.

CENTURY COMPANY: "The Merchants" by Isabell Mackay, copyright 1906; "Make-Believe Town" by Claudia Tharin, copyright 1896.

DODD, MEAD & COMPANY: "Mr. Moon" by Bliss Carman.

DOUBLEDAY, DORAN AND COMPANY: "Animal Crackers" from "Chimneysmoke" by Christopher Morley, copyright 1917 to 1921; "The Fairies Have Never a Penny to Spend" from "Fairies and Chimneys" by Rose Fyleman, copyright 1920; "Very Lovely" and "Vision" from "The Fairy Green" by Rose Fyleman, copyright 1923.

E. P. DUTTON & CO.: "The Edge of the World" from "When We Were Little—Children's Rhymes from Oyster Bay" by Mary Fanny Youngs, copyright 1919.

HEATH CRANTON, Ltd., LONDON: "My Garden," "Rock-a-bye" and "The Door at the End of Our Garden" by Fred E. Weatherly.

HENRY HOLT AND COMPANY: "Some One" by Walter de la Mare from "Collected Poems."

LITTLE, BROWN & COMPANY: "Sunset and Sunrise" by Emily Dickinson.

THE MACMILLAN COMPANY: "Paper Boats" from "Crescent Moon" by Rabindranath Tagore.

SEDGWICK & JACKSON: "Four and Eight" and "Poppies" by Ffrida Wolfe.

FREDERICK A. STOKES: "Fairies," "Adventure," "Tree-Toad" and "Humming-Bird" from "Poems by a Little Girl" by Hilda Conkling, copyright 1920; "Once When We Were Walking" from "For Days and Days" by Annette Wynne, copyright 1919.

THE VIKING PRESS: "Song from 'April'" from "Songs to Save a Soul" by Irene Rutherford McLeod, copyright by B. W. Huebsch, 1919.

153

EDWIN MARKHAM: "A Prayer," used by special permission.

JOHN FARRAR: "The Ambitious Mouse," "Moral Song" and "A Comparison" from "Songs for Parents." Published by Yale University Press.

MARY CAROLYN DAVIES: "After All and After All."

FLORENCE CONVERSE: "A Rune of Riches."

ARTHUR KETCHUM: "The Spirit of the Birch."

BURGES JOHNSON: "Where Dreams are Made" and "Blowing Bubbles" from "Youngsters."

HAMLIN GARLAND: "Do You Fear the Wind."

CLINTON SCOLLARD: "Ducks" and "Daffodil Time."

KATHARINE D. RIGGS: "Mockery."

MARY ELIZABETH RODHOUSE: "To a Tufted Titmouse" and "Off to the Country."

ROBERT GRAVES: "I'd Love to be a Fairy's Child" from "Fairies and Fusiliers."

KATHARINE MORSE: "A Bee Sets Sail" from "A Gate of Cedar."

WILLIAM HARVEY: "The Boy With the Little Bare Toes."

WINIFRED GRAY STEWART: "Summer Rapture."

JOAN ALPERMANN: "A Spring Message."

INDEX OF TITLES

155

156